PORT OF
SOUTHAMPTON

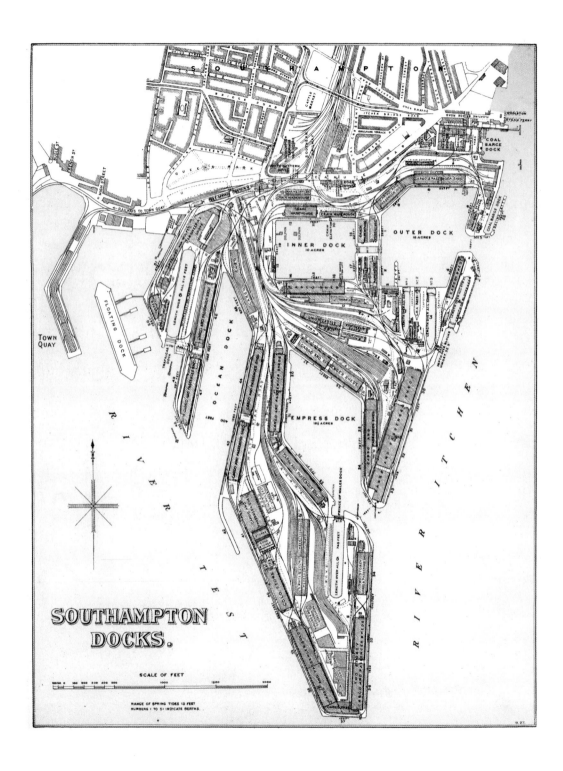

SOUTHAMPTON DOCKS.

SCALE OF FEET

RANGE OF SPRING TIDES 13 FEET
NUMBERS 1 TO 51 INDICATE BERTHS.

PORT OF
SOUTHAMPTON

CAMPBELL McCUTCHEON

AMBERLEY

Frontispiece: Southampton docks in the mid-1920s.

First published 2005, this edition 2008
Amberley Publishing Plc
Cirencester Road, Chalford,
Stroud, Gloucestershire, GL6 8PE
www.amberley-books.com
© Campbell McCutcheon, 2005, 2008

The right of Campbell McCutcheon to be identified as the Author
of this work has been asserted in accordance with the
Copyrights, Designs and Patents Act 1988.

British Library Cataloguing in Publication Data.
A catalogue record for this book is available from the British Library.

ISBN 978 184868 061 6

Printed in Great Britain.

Contents

Acknowledgements

As with all books there are a few people who deserve a special mention and without whom what you read now would not have been possible. Without the many people who have taken the photographs we see here, it would have been impossible to write this book so I would like to thank Mr Courtney, Miss G.A. Pratt, F.G.O. Stuart, C.R. Hoffmann, B.A. Fielden, W.R. Hogg of Ryde, Kirk of Cowes, and the numerous unidentified photographers who have sat at the sides of the Itchen or Test, or at Mayflower Park, or who travelled on the many pleasure steamers and photographed the docks from many angles and whose work is included here. I'd also like to thank my wife, Janette, who helped with the selection of images and who put up with me hiding away in my study writing the book, as well as Rick Cox, Rodney Baker and Tom Stanley, postcard dealers who have managed to find some of the photographic gems you see here. All images are from my collection and represent twenty years of collecting nice shipping images from around the world.

Introduction

Situated in the lee of the Isle of Wight, with four high tides per day, and a good depth of water even at low tide, it comes as no surprise that Southampton has been used as a harbour for many centuries. Its location, close to major markets, has also helped greatly.

There are traces of pre-Roman settlements in the vicinity of the city, and it is safe to say that the ancient Greeks and Phoenicians traded tin in the area too. But it was the Norman conquest of England that saw the rise of Southampton as a port. Trade with the Continent in wine and wool was of great importance to the city. By the fourteenth century trade with the East was established, as was trade with Spain and Genoa. Southampton grew in importance and was one of the leading trading towns in the UK with the Levant.

But what really saw the growth in Southampton's trade with the rest of the world was the granting of an Act of Parliament in 1803 for the construction of docks. It wasn't until 1836 that the Southampton Dock Co. came into being, and a further two years before the foundation stone of the first Southampton docks was laid. From then onwards, the growth in the city's fortunes was dramatic. Population and trade grew at enormous rates and all because of the seemingly never-ending expansion of the dock system, something that still continues to this day.

Growth of Southampton from 1803–1983

Event	Year	Population
The docks first contemplated	1803	8,254
Incorporation of Southampton Dock Co. by Act of Parliament	1836	23,534
Opening of Outer dock	1842	28,500
Opening of Inner dock	1851	35,305
Opening of Old Extension Quay	1875	56,211
Opening of Empress dock	1890	64,405
Transfer of docks to London & South Western Railway	1892	65,621
Itchen Quays developed	1895	
South and Test Quays developed	1902	
Opening of Deep Water Ocean dock	1912	120,512
Population	1921	162,200
New Western docks Extension commenced	1927	
King George V dry dock opened	1933	
Construction of Ocean Terminal	1950	
First Roll-On Roll-Off Ferry terminal at Southampton	1964	
Outer dock rebuilt as Princess Alexandra dock	1967	
Demolition of Ocean Terminal	1983	

By the 1930s, over 15 million tons of shipping were passing annually through the docks, which had by then become the premier passenger port in the UK, as well as a major cargo port.

Even through the Depression the docks were expanded and, in 1932, the Western docks were constructed and a huge area of land reclaimed for new factories (including the Solent Flour Mill). It was at this time that the King George V dry dock, then the largest in the world, was built. The KGV dock could accommodate the largest ships under construction, including Cunard's *Queen Mary*. It nearly wasn't built as the Southern Railway did not want to build the dock as the only ships that were too large at the time to fit in its floating dry dock were the *Queen Mary* and the French Line SS *Normandie*. Quite rightly, the SR did not want to build a special dock for only one ship and it was only the intervention of the Government that saw the construction begin. In July 1933, King George V and Queen Mary sailed the Royal Yacht *Victoria and Albert* into the dock to officially open it. The first ship to use the new repair facility was the RMS *Majestic* of the White Star Line, then the largest ship in the world, in January 1934.

The docks, which had been one of the most important during the First World War, were heavily bombed during the Second. The threat of bombing was constant but Southampton still played a huge part in the D-Day landings and the eventual overthrow of the Germans. By late 1945, liners were beginning to call again, albeit as troopships taking returning soldiers home to the Dominions and the USA. GI Brides often said their last farewells to the UK from Southampton too, and went to the USA, Canada, Australia and New Zealand on fleets of once-luxurious liners such as the *Queen Elizabeth, Mauretania, Aquitania, Queen of Bermuda, Andes* and *Orion*. By 1946, passenger services resumed with the sailings of the *Queen Elizabeth* and she was followed by her older sister *Queen Mary* in 1947. As Britain returned to peace, the damage was made good, and Southampton docks began its growth once more.

In 1950, the Ocean Terminal, one of the most beautiful Art Deco buildings in Southern England, was opened for use. This large passenger terminal helped reinforce Southampton's position as the premier transatlantic passenger port. Southampton saw a mass emigration in the 1950s and 1960s too, as fleets of ships took emigrants to Australia and New Zealand on £10 assisted passages. Lines such as Chandris became as familiar in the docks as Cunard, Shaw Savill, Royal Mail Steam Packet Co., P&O and British India Steam Navigation Co.

By the late 1960s passenger numbers were down, ships like *Queen Mary* and *Queen Elizabeth* were being pensioned off and passenger trade declined sharply as jet aircraft took the largest share of passengers. The 1966 Seamen's Strike also had an adverse effect on the docks as hundreds of thousands of tons of shipping were laid up for the duration. Those passengers that still used passenger ships were soon deserting the liners for the speedier jet airliners. During the 1970s, while cargo trade was on the up, the last Union Castle mail runs to South Africa were operated, ships like *Canberra* stopped undertaking line voyages and moved entirely to cruising, and even Cunard sold off most of its fleet to concentrate on cargo ships and cruising. In 1974 the SS *France* stopped her transatlantic crossings too, leaving only the QE2 as the last transatlantic liner. Union Castle made its last South African mail run in 1977, while *Canberra* had gone over entirely to cruising by 1975.

Freight traffic had been growing though, mainly as a result of containerisation and the import of motor vehicles into Southampton. The docks themselves were one of the early homes of Elders & Fyffes, the first company to import bananas in large quantities to the UK, and there is still a major fruit terminal in the Western docks next to Mayflower

Park. Fawley Refinery was also important and still sees oil tankers of various sizes calling to offload cargoes of oil.

Ferries, as always, played a major role in the docks, and not just the Red Funnel and other pleasure steamers from the Town Quay and Royal Pier. There were services to the Isle of Wight and also to Le Havre and Cherbourg. In 1967 the Princess Alexandra dock was opened for roll-on roll-off ferries on the site of the old Outer docks, which had been derelict for a few years. Unfortunately, apart from the Red Funnel service to the Isle of Wight and the Hythe Ferry, the ferry services have gone to Portsmouth, and all cross-channel sailings are now from there instead.

In the past two decades, Southampton has seen a resurgence in passenger services but now the ships are cruise ships, calling at a myriad of European destinations from the North Cape to the Baltic, Mediterranean and Atlantic Islands, as well as the transatlantic services of Cunard. The port is now the busiest passenger port in the UK once more, with over 250 ship calls per annum. P&O and Cunard ships are still a regular sight, but they have been joined by vessels from Royal Caribbean, Norwegian Cruise Line, Princess Cruises, Saga Cruises and Voyages of Discovery, instead of the likes of Union Castle, Orient Line, British India and a host of other lines that have totally disappeared from the world of shipping.

One of the biggest tragedies of the past twenty years was the loss of the Ocean Terminal, destroyed by institutionalised vandals who foresaw no future use for the most beautiful passenger terminal of any major port and who ordered its demolition. The beautiful Art Deco building was pulled down and its site has lain derelict save for the use of the dockside to load scrap metal. Ocean Quay itself also lies unused now and it is sad to reflect that the dock (opened in 1911) will probably never see another passenger vessel. *Calshot*, the sole surviving passenger tender, lies awaiting an uncertain future too. Now in the care of Southampton City Council, it is unlikely that she will ever be restored as the council do not have the funds to preserve her.

The KGV dry dock is still used on a regular basis and Southampton is seeing huge growth as a cargo port again, although the decision not to build a new container terminal at Dibden is surely a sign that there will be little further expansion in the docks over the next few decades.

The story of the port of Southampton is the story of the city itself. Without the docks, it is doubtful if Southampton would be as important a settlement as it is today. From those small beginnings in the 1800s has grown Britain's premier passenger port, an accolade the city still holds today – long may it continue!

I hope that you enjoy the following pages, and I apologise now if I have not managed to include a picture of your favourite ship or to cover adequately in pictures the development and growth of the dock system at Southampton. I have tried to use, wherever possible, images that have never seen the light of day before but I'm sure that amongst them are some old favourites, used as I have found no alternative. I have tried wherever possible to illustrate ships photographed at Southampton itself, and if this has led to some well-known vessels being omitted, I apologise.

Overleaf: The sailing vessel *Pamir* at Southampton's Western docks in 1939 after she had arrived with 4,300 tons of wheat from Australia. She arrived from Port Victoria in ninety-six days, arriving on 26 June 1939 on what was to be the last grain race before the war. After delivery to the Solent flour mills, she left again on 21 July, sailing for Gothenburg.

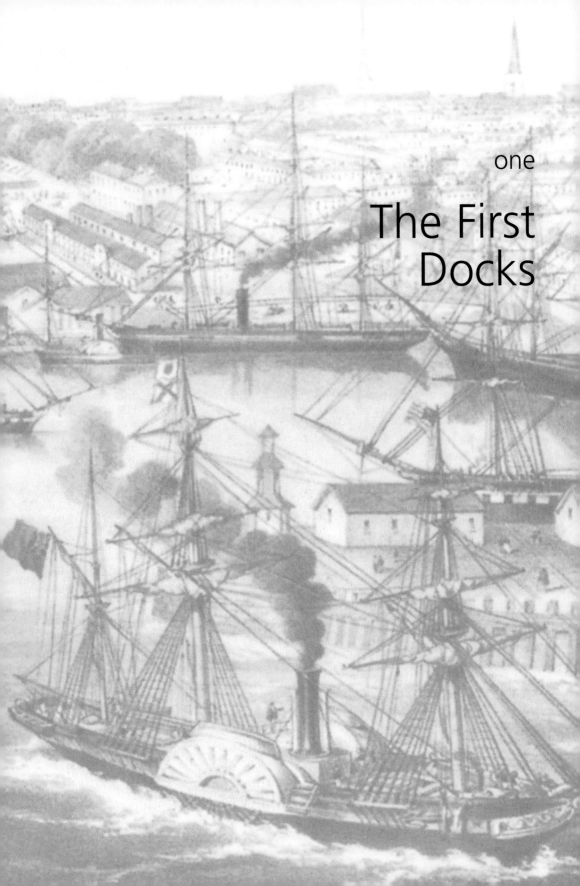

one

The First
Docks

Prior to the 1830s, Southampton's trade was mainly coastal or short continental, and those piers that were used were often dry at low tide. The one exception was the Royal Victoria Pier which had only opened in 1833, and which was unsuitable for the larger vessels then under construction. It was with great foresight that the founding fathers of the port of Southampton submitted a Bill to Parliament for the construction of the first Southampton docks. They laid the foundation for the third largest port in the UK and of the country's largest passenger port. In 1836 the Southampton Dock Co. had purchased 216 acres of marsh and mudlands adjoining the Town Quay, for which they paid the princely sum of £5,000.

The foundation stone of the new docks was actually laid on 12 October 1838, and construction began apace with Francis Giles as Engineer. His son, Alfred, served the Southampton Dock Co. as Engineer from 1846, when his father died.

At the time of the construction of the new dock, a revolution was happening. Steam had begun to prove itself as a motive power for ships and the Government had begun to issue contracts for the regular carriage of mail by steamship. The companies founded at this time were to play a major part in the history of the port over the ensuing decades. They were to include the Peninsular & Oriental Steam Navigation Co., the Royal Mail Steam Packet Co. and the British & North American Steam Packet Co. (which would become famous as the Cunard Line).

On 11 May 1840, the railway line from London Nine Elms to Southampton was opened for traffic and this line, the London & South Western Railway, was also to play an important part in the history of the docks. The coming of the steamship had seen the Southampton Dock Co.'s directors change their plans and they built a tidal dock rather than the closed dock that had been proposed. It opened to its first steamships, the P&O liners RMS *Tagus* (780 tons) and *Liverpool* (450 tons) on 29 August 1842, with a direct rail connection across Canute Road to the ships' sides. Cargo was unloaded direct from the ships to the waiting freight wagons and was delivered to London on the same day. Barely a year later, on 1 July 1841, the dock opened for general traffic.

The founding of the Royal Mail Steam Packet Co. (RMSP) in 1839, and the decision of its directors based on a report by the famous engineer John Smeaton to use Southampton as its British base, led to almost 150 years of RMSP ships using the port. Between 1846 and 1853, the Southampton Dock Co. also constructed three dry docks. The first opened on 27 July 1846 with the RMSP vessel *Forth* (1,939 tons) entering to have her wooden hull sheathed in copper (which was used to prevent the boring of the Teredo worm). The 1840s and 1850s were a period of huge growth in British shipping and new technological developments such as iron hulls and screw propellers saw their introduction into new ship design. The Southampton Dock Co. had realised that steam was the way to go and that it had to expand and in 1851, the Inner dock was opened. But, in 1854, with the beginning of the Crimean War, British trade and shipbuilding was to go into decline as the Government commandeered many of the ships of the merchant marine as troopships, hospital ships and cargo vessels. The port was used as a major base for the transport of troops, cargo, coal and horses for the Crimea and, with the increasing size of vessels, the Inner dock had to have its entrance widened from 46ft and its depth increased to cope with the extra traffic using the port. Work was completed on 25 May 1859, with the P&O RMS *Persia* being the first ship to use the new deepened Inner dock.

The docks were also beginning to be used as a regular port of call for continental transatlantic steamers too and in 1857 the first Hamburg Amerika liner called, followed a year later by the first North German Lloyd ship.

Further expansion was required and, in 1873, construction began of new quays along the river Itchen frontage, extending for over 2,000ft. In 1875, P&O changed their main UK port to London and Southampton lost much trade. Despite this, traffic through the port rose in 1876. Three years later, the next dry dock, the fourth in the port, was opened on the river Itchen.

Despite a global depression in the early 1880s, the Southampton Dock Co., with money borrowed from the LSWR, began construction on reclaimed land of what would become the Empress dock. The extra 3,800ft of frontage was important for three reasons. The first and most obvious was that it again hugely expanded Southampton's dock area, while the second was that it provided yet another dry dock (capable of accommodating the ever-increasing size of vessels). The third reason was most important: Southampton had now become the only port in the whole of Great Britain at which any ship, regardless of size and draught, could be accommodated and berthed at any state of the tide. The future looked good for the port and the town.

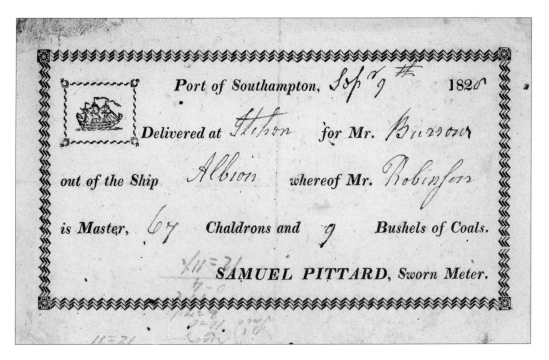

A waybill from 9 September 1820 for sixty-seven chaldrons and nine bushels of coal delivered at Itchen for Mr Burrows out of the sailing vessel *Albion*. Scribbled on the back is the account for the unloading of the coal. Interestingly, the discharge and unloading cost £1 14s 2d in labour.

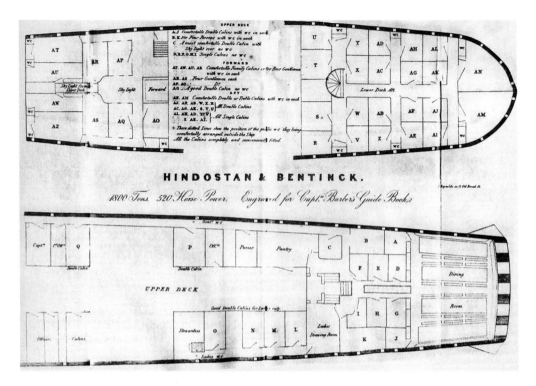

The P&O RMS *Hindustan* sailed from Southampton on her maiden voyage on 24 September 1842. She left for the Cape and Calcutta, before commencing sailings to and from Suez. This deck plan shows just how small she was. Only eight of the sixty cabins on board had private toilets.

A bill from Southampton Wharf from 13 December 1821 to W. Burrowes [sic] of the sailing vessel *Nancy* for one bag of ironmongery.

Opposite below: A carte de visite published by Symonds & Gyngell of Manchester Street and Shirley Road, Southampton, of the RMSP ship *Nile*. The RMS *Nile* was to become the Union Steamship Co.'s *German*. The Union Steamship Co. had been founded immediately prior to the Crimean War to transport coal to the Mediterranean but soon grew to become the mail line to South Africa.

Above: The docks in 1854–56, showing clearly the Inner and Outer docks, with the original three dry-dock entrances to the left of the picture. Ships of both P&O and RMSP are in dock, and the paddler steaming up the Itchen is likely going to the Northam repair yards.

Regular Line of United States Mail Steam Packets between New York and Bremen, via Southampton.

THE OCEAN STEAM
U. S. MAIL
WASHINGTON

NAVIGATION COMPANY'S
STEAM SHIPS
AND HERMANN

depart from BREMEN and SOUTHAMPTON for NEW YORK

AT THE FOLLOWING DATES:—

The "WASHINGTON," Captain Johnston,

FROM BREMEN	FROM SOUTHAMPTON
On the 15th February,	On the 20th February,
On the 15th April,	On the 20th April,
On the 15th June,	On the 20th June,

The "HERMANN," Captain Crabtree,

FROM BREMEN	FROM SOUTHAMPTON
On the 15th March,	On the 20th March,
On the 15th May,	On the 20th May,
On the 15th July,	On the 20th July,

PASSAGE, payable in advance.

First Class Thirty Guineas ; including all charges, except for Wines and Liquors to be obtained of the Steward, and which Passengers are not permitted to take on board.

No Second Class or Steerage Passengers are taken. Servants, and Children under ten years, half-price.

Stewards' Fees at the discretion of Passengers. Dogs £5 each, and 10s. Steward's Fees for feeding.

Passengers' Baggage to be on board the day previous to sailing. Half a Ton *personal* Baggage allowed each Passenger paying full fare. Merchandize taken as Baggage, will be charged the highest rate of Freight.

Berths only secured by payment of the full Passage Money, half of which will be returned to Passengers not proceeding.

FREIGHTS, payable in New York.

25 to 35 dollars per Ton measurement, according to quality and quantity.

Specie, half per cent ; Watches, and Jewellery, one per cent. on the value.

Primage, in all cases, 5 per cent. No Bill of Lading signed for a less freight than 5 dollars.

No Goods will be shipped from Southampton, unless delivered there on or before the 16th of the month, with proper advice for Entry addressed to the undersigned, with whom all engagements for freight must be made.

Railway and Shipping Charges on Goods and Specie, forwarded through the undersigned will be paid by him, if desired, charged in the Bill of Lading and collected in *New York*, at the rate of 4.80 dollars to the £ Sterling.

PARCELS and Small Packages

for all parts of the United States and Canada will be received in LONDON until Noon of the days previous to sailing, by Mr. JOHN MILLER, U.S. Despatch Agent, 26, Henrietta-Street, Covent Garden ; or at 57, Threadneedle-street ; and forwarded to NEW YORK at the following rates, which must be pre-paid.

	Weighing under 5lbs.,	Measurement under ¼ Cubic Foot..							5s. 0d.
	" " 7lbs.,	" " ¼ "	..	..	..	..	..	7s. 6d.
	" " 10lbs.,	" " ½ "	..	..	..	..	..	10s. 0d.
	" " 14lbs.,	" " 1 "	..	..	..	..	..	12s. 6d.
	" " 21lbs.,	" " 1 "	..	..	..	..	..	15s. 0d.
	" " 28lbs.,	" " 1 "	..	..	..	..	..	20s. 0d.

Rates from London to New York.

Every additional lb. weight to pay 6d.; Parcels exceeding 1 cubic foot measurement to be shipped by Bill of Lading. It is optional to charge the above rates either by weight or measurement.

From NEW YORK Parcels will be forwarded by Messrs. HARNDEN & Co., at moderate charges, to be paid by the Consignees.

For Freight or Passage apply to Messrs. C. A. HEINEKEN and Co., BREMEN ; Mr. WM. ISELIN, HAVRE ; Messrs. DRAPER & Co., PARIS ; Mr. EDWARD STAINER, 57, Threadneedle-street, LONDON ; or to the undersigned

JOSEPH RODNEY CROSKEY,
U. S. Consul. Southampton.

The Ocean Steam Navigation Co.'s US Mail Steam Ships *Washington* and *Hermann* called at the port in 1848 on their journey from Bremerhaven to New York. From Bremerhaven to Southampton took five days while passage was thirty guineas for first-class passengers. Servants were half price and dogs were carried at the cost of £5 each. Their feeding was an extra 10*s*. In a far cry from today's allowances on an aircraft, personal baggage allowance was a full ½ ton. The return journey from Bremerhaven-Southampton-New York-Bremerhaven was scheduled to take a full two months.

The Inner dock, c.1900, with various ships in port including the Castle Line vessels *Northam Castle* (second from left) and *Roslin Castle* (fourth). The *Roslin Castle* has had her funnel lengthened in this view.

The Union Line's *Scot* as built and shown here in Southampton Water. She was lengthened considerably later in her career, while her funnels were shortened. She was of 6,850grt and undertook the express mail service to the Cape. When the Boer War started she was commandeered for trooping and was, until the advent of the RMS *Norman*, the largest ship of the fleet.

22 & 21 OXFORD STREET, SOUTHAMPTON (One minute from Entrance to Docks)   P.T.O.

There were numerous photographers associated with the port of Southampton. Amongst them were names like F.G.O. Stuart, C.R. and O.V. Hoffmann, Thomas Adams and G.A. Pratt. Here is Miss G.A. Pratt's shop in Oxford Street, barely a minute from the entrance to the docks.

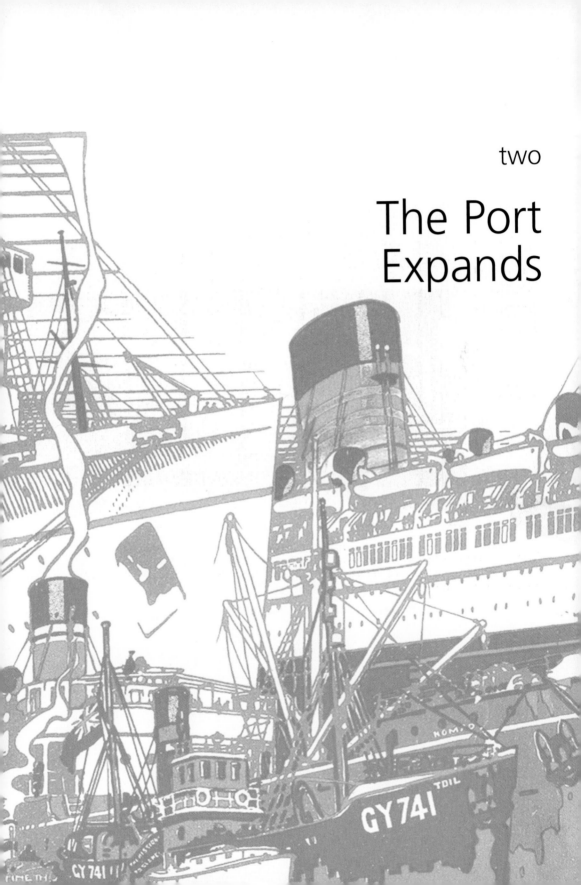

two

The Port
Expands

In 1892, the Southampton Dock Co. was sold to the London & South Western Railway and a new period of expansion began. The Itchen Quays were the first evidence of the money that poured into the city as a result of the LSWR purchase of the docks and were completed originally as the Prince of Wales quays, and were the home of the Union Castle Mail Steamship Company. In 1902, the Test Quays and South Quay were opened for traffic. The South Quay was originally used for the Rotterdam Lloyd and Nederland Royal Mail lines for services to the Netherlands East Indies, but by the 1920s were used mainly by the Union Castle Line. On the Test Quay was the warehouse of the International Cold Storage Co., one of the largest refrigerated warehouses in the UK. The Trafalgar graving dock was opened in 1905.

With the transfer of the White Star Line express service from Liverpool to Southampton in 1907, there was a need for a new dock and construction began of the 15½-acre White Star dock. It opened partially in mid-1911 to accommodate the *Olympic*, and opened fully later that year. It was from the White Star dock that the *Titanic* left on her fateful maiden voyage. In 1922, the White Star dock was renamed the Ocean dock because of the fact that Cunard Line and United States Line ships were using the dock also. In 1924, a new floating dock was built and a common sight from the dock offices or Royal Pier was a huge liner lifted out of the water, a process that took about eight-ten hours from start to finish.

By the late 1920s it was obvious that the docks would need to be extended again, and work began on the Western Extension to the port. In 1932 Cunard's *Mauretania* became the first ship to use the new extension. With the new quays, a new graving dock was also constructed to accommodate the new Cunard liner 534, under construction at Clydebank. Opened in 1933 by King George V and Queen Mary, the first ship to use the dry dock was the *Majestic* in January 1934.

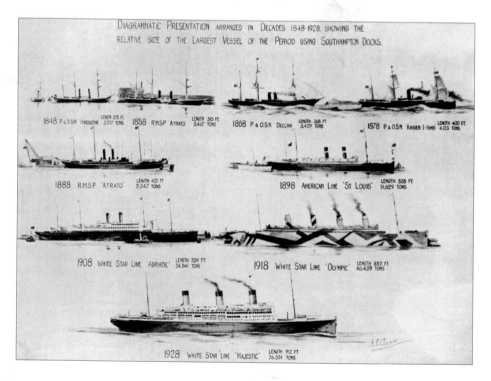

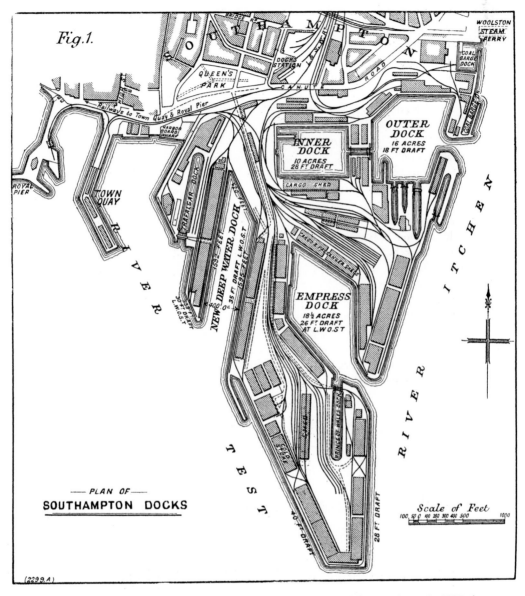

Southampton docks in 1911, showing the new White Star dock and the Test Quays. In 1905, the Trafalgar dry dock was opened, but only six years later it was already being rebuilt to take larger vessels.

Opposite: A diagrammatic representation of why the docks had to grow in size. From 1848 to 1923, the size of ships had grown by twenty-eight times. By 1936, the *Queen Mary* was forty times larger than the typical ship of 1848.

The Outer dock, with an American Line ship (USMS *St Paul*) in dock. Her funnel is being painted and she has tarpaulins draped along her promenade deck to ensure that coal dust does not enter the passenger areas as she is being coaled.

Grain warehouse in the Inner dock, showing the elevator equipment used to remove the grain from ships. The ship is the *Navarchos C. Sachtouris*. The grain elevator could handle eighty tons per hour and electric conveyors could carry the grain to any part of the warehouses.

South African produce in one of the warehouses on the Test Quays.

Discharging timber at No.41 Berth on the Test Quay.

A Goliath crane in action. These cranes were located at the back of Nos 34–36 sheds and could carry loads of up to one ton.

With the announcement that the White Star Line was to build two new superliners, the *Olympic* and *Titanic*, it was also announced that a new dock would be built in Southampton to service the two behemoths. The new dock was opened in time for *Olympic*'s entry to service in June 1911 and was 1,700ft long and 400ft wide. This view shows the excavation work in June 1908.

The site of the dock was mudflats that had been used for tipping ashes from ships' boilers and it was separated from the River Test by a porous chalk bank. This was made watertight and excavation work began behind this bank. Excavation was undertaken to 30ft below sea level.

April 1909, and the trench and timbering for the quay walls is under construction.

In the background can be seen some of the completed quay wall with timber shuttering being constructed to extend this quay wall. This view is from March 1910.

The North East berth in May 1911. From 800-1,200 men were continuously employed building the new dock over a period of four years. Twenty divers set concrete blocks into the foundations below sea level.

Opposite below: The White Star dock, soon after its opening. In dock are two American Line vessels, a White Star ship, most likely *Adriatic*, and an RMSP liner.

Above: A view of No.22 berth taken during the First World War. At this time, the warehouse was used to accommodate wounded soldiers as they came off hospital ships to be shipped by ambulance train to VAD hospitals throughout the UK.

Above: The Royal Pier was used by the many pleasure steamers that called at Southampton, as well as by the Red Funnel paddle steamers to the Isle of Wight. On a summer Saturday there would be perhaps four or five paddle steamers using the pier at any one time.

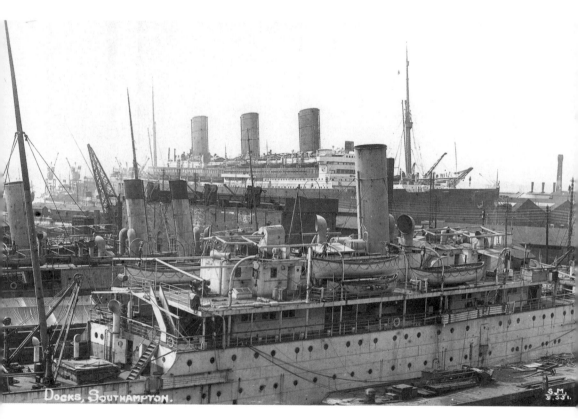

DOCKS, SOUTHAMPTON.

Above: Looking into the White Star dock in the late 1920s with Cunard's *Berengaria* on the left. Construction work is being undertaken on the South Western Hotel, which was Southampton's premier hotel, and this dates the image to *c.*1928. It was here that first-class passengers often stayed overnight before their travels.

Right: The Royal Mail Steam Packet Co.'s RMS *Trent* of 1899. Her main claim to fame was that she rescued the crew of the airship *America* in 1910, when the airship was trying to make the first crossing of the Atlantic by air.

Opposite below: Looking over to the White Star dock, with the Hamburg Amerika liner *Imperator* in dock. When built, she was the largest ship in the world, and she made her maiden voyage in April 1913. This view has been taken before her funnels were shortened (to lose weight from the top-heavy ship) but after she had lost the huge eagle figurehead on her bow.

S.S.BERENGARIA BEING TOWED OUT, SOUTHAMPTON DOCK.

91864.JV

Berengaria being towed out of the Ocean dock, as the White Star dock was renamed in the early 1920s. Her sister ship, White Star's *Majestic*, is to the right. Both ships were war reparations from Germany and had been built for the Hamburg Amerika line.

Union Castle's RMS *Kenilworth Castle* at No.39 berth on the Test Quay, just along from the International Cold Store. RMS *Kenilworth Castle* was launched on 15 December 1903, and scrapped in 1936.

Viewed on the same day at Berth 41 is the Canadian Pacific Line's RMS *Empress of Canada*. This view shows her on 18 September 1929, when she made one trip from Southampton to Quebec before returning via the Panama Canal to her normal Vancouver station for transpacific service. In 1943 she was torpedoed and sunk in the South Atlantic.

In 1924, Southampton acquired a floating dry dock – the largest in the world. The Prince of Wales opened the dry dock and the first ship to use it, in June 1924, was the Union Castle Line's RMS *Windsor Castle*. Here, White Star's *Olympic* is shown photographed from Cunard's *Mauretania* at some point in the mid-1920s.

By the late 1920s, despite the international recession, it was obvious that Southampton's docks would have to grow again. It was decided that the mudflats along the river Test would be reclaimed and a new dock opened on a new 407-acre site. The original plan was that there were to be two graving docks at the end of the new development but, after discussions with the Cunard Line, it was decided to build a single large graving dock. This view shows work underway on the construction of the new quay wall.

Above: An aerial view looking from above the Royal Pier, showing the extent of the reclamation work. Work on the quay wall is well underway. The site of Mayflower Park is being used as a base for the construction work. Once the quay wall was built, the mudflats behind were reclaimed by pumping the water out and the new warehouses were built. This view was taken on 1 November 1929.

Right: The first ship to use the new dock extension, which extended to as far as Millbrook, was the *Mauretania* in 1932. Here she is seen in mid-1933, painted white for cruising and dressed overall in flags.

Opposite below: The new quays extended to over 7,000ft, and one of the main advantages for ship spotters and residents of Southampton was the construction of Mayflower Park. Here, work continues on the building of the quay wall. A White Star liner can be seen in the background.

NEW DOCKS, MILLBROOK, SOUTHAMPTON. 41

Above: Viewed from next to the entrance gate to the dock. Behind the crane is one of the water inlets for filling the dock up again.

Right: The huge dock gate inside the Prince of Wales dry dock, being readied for installation.

Opposite above: Orient Line's *Orontes* or *Oronsay* berthed at Millbrook in the mid-1930s. These ships often cruised from Southampton in the 1930s. Grain for the Solent Flour Mills is most likely the cargo of the MV *Berent*.

Opposite below: Construction work underway on the King George V graving dock in 1932-33. This view shows work underway on the excavation of the dock.

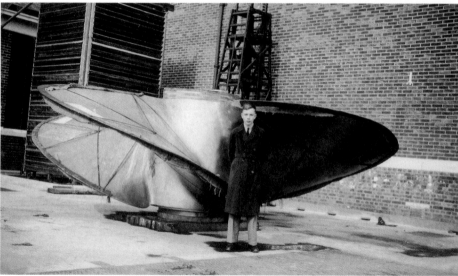

Above: The *Queen Mary*, seen here in late March 1936 as she made her first ever visit to the dry dock to be painted and have her hull checked over for the first time. Each one of her propellers weighed over 35 tons.

Opposite top: The dock gate was installed in this space. Opposite, and to the right, is the steel framework for the pumping house. It could empty the dry dock in a few hours and, at 1,200ft long, the dock could accommodate the largest ships in the world.

Opposite middle: Looking from Hythe, one of the Union Castle four-stackers is berthed at No.36 with a RMSP motor ship (most likely RMS *Asturias*), behind her.

Opposite bottom: This turn of the century view shows the docks from Southampton Water, with the sailing ship *Hurst Castle* and a Union Castle liner.

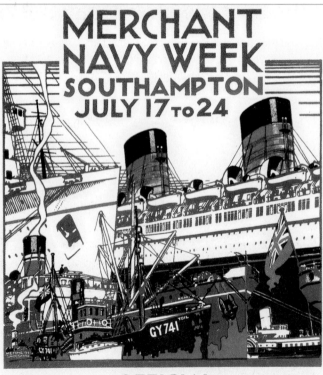

Above: It is more unusual to see views taken from Woolston, looking up the Itchen to the docks. Here, Canadian Pacific's RMS *Empress of Britain* towers majestically over the docks, dating the photo to the early 1930s, soon after she was built.

Left: A regular occurrence through the 1930s was Merchant Navy Week. In 1937, HMS *Renown* and HMS *Southampton* visited for the event which was held at berths Nos 107 and 108. Cunard's *Aquitania* was open for inspection at 1*s* per head and there were displays showing how Britain could not manage without her merchant navy. The cover of the souvenir programme was drawn by Kenneth Shoesmith, one of Britain's foremost marine artists.

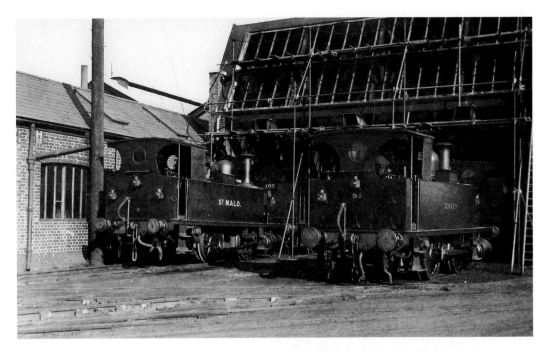

The docks were owned by the railway company and had their own engine shed for the many shunting engines that moved wagons around the dock system. Here is the engine shed in April 1938, with the 0-4-0 shunters *Jersey* and *St Malo*. These small shunters could easily move carriages and wagons around the tight curves found in parts of the docks.

Here, *Granville* sits outside Berth No.43 with the RMS *Queen Mary* towering over the sheds. This view dates from 1936, just before the maiden voyage of *Queen Mary*.

Above aand below: Two more of the Southampton docks shunters, *Alderney* and *Cherbourg*. The locomotives were designed by Adams and Drummond and were built between 1891 and 1908 and were classified by the LSWR as B.4. Fourteen of the class were delivered to Southampton docks and were given names of ports served by Southampton and the LSWR. Most of the class were scrapped by 1948 with only three survivors by 1961.

Another of the class shunts wagons alongside White Star's *Homeric*. They were supplanted by a class of fourteen 0-6-0s purchased by the Southern Railway in 1947 from the War Department.

A busy view of the docks in the mid-1930s with Blue Star Line's *Arandora Star*, Cunard's *Aquitania* and the tugs *Sloyne* and *Wellington*. *Arandora Star* was converted for cruising and was one of the most luxurious cruise ships of her time.

The war had a major effect on Southampton and after the war, the city once more became the premier transatlantic port. To cope with the traffic, a new passenger terminal was built – the Ocean Terminal. This beautiful Art Deco building was begun in 1948 and completed in 1950.

The tower at the seaward end served a valuable purpose, housing customs officials and as an area for bonded baggage. The terminal was ¼ mile long and was built in two storeys (one for baggage and the other for passengers). The Ocean Terminal was opened by Clement Attlee on 31 July 1950.

It was in May 1946 that the decision to build the terminal took place. A party of dock officials stood in the shattered bomb-site that had been the Cunard White Star terminal and planned the construction of the new terminal. The Fine Arts Commission approved the design of the Art Deco terminal and work began in early 1948.

In 1983, institutionalised vandals decided that the terminal had to come down and Southampton lost one of its premier buildings. It is sad to reflect that, as the city grows again as the premier passenger port in the UK, it has lost the glamorous Ocean Terminal, which could have been such an attraction.

Left and opposite above: Major alteration works took place in the 1950s and 1960s as the docks were rebuilt to cope with changed market and trade conditions. The Inner docks were filled in and a new ferry terminal built in what was the Outer docks. The dock was renamed the Princess Alexandra dock and provided a roll-on/roll-off ferry service to France and Spain. These two views show the amount of work undertaken to reclaim the land for the terminal. The latter view dates from March 1967.

Opposite below: It is 4 March 1975 and Townsend Thoresen's ferry *Viking 1* leaves the ferry terminal.

Looking over the old Harland & Wolff works and the Trafalgar graving dock, this view illustrates just how much the Inner dock area had changed by 1976. It was again to be altered when the Princess Alexandra dock was closed and parts of this area converted to housing. At the end of the H&W sheds can be seen the old entrance to the docks and what was once the shop of C.R. Hoffmann, the famous postcard publisher.

three

Ship Repair
and Building

As with all major ports, ship building and repair has been an important function of the docks in Southampton. From the earliest days there have been shipyards in Northam, while dry, or graving, docks have been an important function of the original docks in Southampton. With ocean-going steamships using the port from the beginning, the provision of ship-repair facilities has been an important function and a necessity. By the 1930s, Southampton had a repair facility second to none – with a collection of dry docks that could take even the largest of ocean liners. The 1,200ft-long King George V graving dock was the largest dry dock in the world when it was built. The docks' floating dock was also the largest in the world when it was built and, until the advent of the *Queen Mary*, could cope with the largest vessel at the time. As well as Thorneycroft, whose yards could build ships of up to 6,500 tons, Southampton boasted a ship-repair facility belonging to Harland & and another belonging to J. Samuel White, of Cowes. As well as repair work on the many ships of the White Star Line, the Southampton works also built many interior fittings for ocean liners such as the *Olympic* and *Titanic*.

A surprising amount of ships have been built in the city as well as oil rigs, paddle steamers, tugs, motor launches, and other small craft.

Work undertaken on ships includes the rebuilding of the *Monarch of Bermuda* into the Shaw Savill liner *New Australia* after the former caught fire and was burned out. Thorneycroft also undertook the conversion of RMS *Majestic* into the navy training ship HMS *Caledonia*. Annual overhauls of famous liners such as *Queen Mary*, *Queen Elizabeth*, *Olympic*, *Aquitania* and *Mauretania* could also be witnesses in the docks. While the days of the great liners are gone, repair work is still undertaken in Southampton and the King George V dry dock often has a vessel under annual overhaul or repair.

Opposite above: Shipbuilding at Northam, *c*.1905.

Opposite below: The Norddeutscher Lloyd liner *Deutschland* in the Trafalgar dry dock, *c*.1905.

Above: Perhaps the most famous Northam yard was Thorneycroft. As well as the yard at Northam, they had a factory at Basingstoke, which made trucks. This advert postcard dates from the 1920s and shows a Thorneycroft–built 40ft cruiser on the Norfolk Broads.

Left: Thorneycroft also undertook much repair work in Southampton and could build ships of up to 6,500 tons. They built many naval vessels as well as merchant ships.

Oppostie below: One of the major feats of engineering at the turn of the twentieth century was the salvage and rebuilding of White Star's vessel SS *Suevic*. This ship, a veteran of the Australian route, was wrecked off the Lizard Point in Cornwall. Her bow was blown off with explosives where she lay and the stern section, aft of the bridge, was towed to Southampton for rebuilding and fitting of a new bow.

Above: The bow was built at Harland & Wolff, in Belfast, and has the distinction of being one of the very few ships to have been launched bow first (to protect the temporary bulkhead that would be removed when the two halves were knitted together again). The bow is shown here in 1908, sandwiched between the RMS *Avon* and RMS *Danube* of the Royal Mail Steam Packet Co.

Above: The two halves of *Suevic* were knitted together by Harland & Wolff and she then sailed with White Star until 1928, when she was converted into a whale factory ship. She was sunk in Norway in 1940 during the invasion of the country by the Nazis.

Above: Dutch liner *Limburgia* of the Royal Holland Lloyd Line in the Trafalgar dry dock, *c.*1916. Of 19,582 tons, she was purchased by United American Lines in 1922. Named *Reliance*, she was registered in Panama to circumvent the Volstead Prohibition Act and sold to HAPAG in 1926. The name painted on her side was to ensure that German submarines would not try and sink her as she was from neutral Holland.

Above: Right: This one wasn't in for a refit. With obvious bow damage, this ship is being repaired, after collision, in August 1928 in one of the smaller dry docks. J. Samuel White used the Prince of Wales dry dock for repair work.

Opposite below: Holland America Line's *Rotterdam* in No.5 dry dock, April 1912.

Above: In 1929, NDL's *Bremen* came to visit for repair. An unusual occurrence, she came only the one time and that was due to the fact that her sister ship *Europa* had been badly damaged by fire while fitting out and the available dry dock in Germany was being used by *Europa*. Burned out herself in 1942 (probably by a disgruntled crew member), she was scrapped where she lay, at Bremerhaven.

Above: Mauretania has had her rudder removed prior to removal of her propellers during a January 1927 refit. The propeller being removed has had a tip broken off.

Right: A crankshaft is loaded aboard Cunard's *Aquitania,* in 1929. The mammoth floating crane lifting the crankshaft could carry up to 150 tons and it was possible to move it anywhere within the dock system. It did also sail to the Isle of Wight at least once, loaded with new carriages for the railway line there.

Opposite below: Cunard's *Aquitania,* all 45,647 tons of her, high and dry on the floating dry dock, which was purchased in 1924. The floating dry dock could lift the largest ship in the world at the time and it took about eight hours for the operation to be performed. The dry dock was opened officially by the Prince of Wales (who became Edward VIII) and the first ship to be lifted was *Windsor Castle.* In the 1930s, after the King George V graving dock was built, the dry dock was sold to the Admiralty and moved to Portsmouth.

A super view taken from *Mauretania* in 1928, showing *Olympic* on her annual refit. The mammoth crane is on the right.

The SS *Windsor Castle*, the twelfth and penultimate four stacker to be built, in the Trafalgar dry dock *c.*1930, with *Aquitania* behind her in what had previously been the White Star dock but what had become by the 1920s the Ocean dock. *Windsor Castle* saw a huge rebuild in the 1930s which saw her gain a new bow and lose two smokestacks. She was bombed in 1943 and sunk off Algiers during an air attack.

AIRCRAFT TENDER
Built of Birmabright by Birmal Boats, Southampton

Finished throughout with "RYLARD" and "OGLOSO"

An aircraft tender constructed at Southampton by Birmal Boats. This would have been used to service flying boats.

The Birmal tender would have been used to tender a flying boat such as this one at Calshot. This RAF plane is being passed by the Red Star Line ship, SS *Belgenland*, a common visitor in the 1920s and early 1930s. *Belgenland* was built by Harland & Wolff at Belfast and served as *Belgic* for White Star before joining Red Star Line. She was scrapped at Bo'ness as the *Columbia* of Panama Pacific Line.

Canadian Pacific's RMS *Empress of Britain* enters the floating dry dock for a refit. She was a dual-purpose ship, designed for summer service to Quebec in Canada and for luxurious world tours in the winter. For her world tours, two of her propellers were removed and she sailed round the world at a leisurely seventeen knots. *Empress of Britain* was registered in London but never sailed there. She was sunk off the coast of Ireland by the Germans and was the biggest merchant loss of the Second World War.

Cunard's *Berengaria* being towed into the floating dry dock in the late 1920s. The old Trafalgar dry dock had a small nick added to the end so that *Berengaria* could be overhauled there. She managed to fit with less than a foot to spare. There were no problems fitting in the floating dock.

In 1936, the White Star liner *Majestic*, once the largest ship in the world, was sold by Cunard White Star for scrap. Her new owner, Sir John Jarvis MP, then sold her on to HM Government for conversion to a training ship, HMS *Caledonia*. Here, she lies at Southampton's Western docks after the auction of her fittings but before conversion had begun. To be located at Rosyth, her masts were to be cut down along with the tops of her funnels, so that she could fit under the Forth Rail Bridge.

In March 1936, Britain's **most** famous and largest liner sailed from Clydebank to Southampton to be docked in the graving dock. Her keel cleaned of the silt of eighteen months of fitting out at Clydebank, she sailed on a series of trials, then left on her maiden voyage in May 1936, taking the Blue Riband from the French Line's *Normandie* soon afterwards.

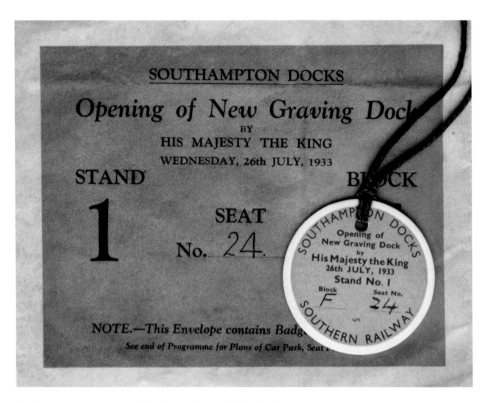

An invite to the opening of the King George V dry dock.

Of course, smaller ships were repaired at Southampton too. Here, in the Prince of Wales dry dock are two of Cosens of Weymouth's fleet of paddle steamers. Photographed on 29 April 1954, *Monarch* and *Embassy* are near the end of a winter refit.

Above and below: The Furness Bermuda Line SS *Monarch of Bermuda* was burned out at the end of the Second World War. She was taken to Southampton to Thorneycroft and rebuilt. As can be seen in the top picture, she was cut down to her hull and rebuilt totally, such was the desperate need for shipping post-war. She was rebuilt as *New Australia* and operated by the Shaw Savill Line as an emigrant ship, taking people on the £10 assisted passage to the Antipodes. It was a far cry from her early days on the New York–Bermuda run and the standard of comfort for the Australian emigrants was far short of that for the American millionaires on the four-day Bermuda run.

S.S. NEW AUSTRALIA.

Not all ship repairs were successful – here the Great Western Railway passenger tender *Sir John Hawkins* burns while under repair in dry dock in January 1952. She was built as a tug/tender for Plymouth docks in 1929 at Earle's shipyard at Hull and was 939 tons gross and was the largest tender in the GWR fleet at 172½ft long.

Workers leave Harland & Wolff at some point in the mid-1930s.

Above and below: In 1959, Steel Structures Ltd built the first mobile oil drilling platform at Southampton. Named *Orient Explorer* it was destined for British North Borneo and was towed there during January and February 1959, a distance of some 9,000 miles. It was completely self-contained and had accommodation for fifty-six men and was built to withstand winds of 100mph.

The paddle steamer *Duchess of Cornwall* is tucked away behind some of the buoys and small ships of the Southampton Harbour Board on 19 June 1949.

Queen Mary, on 3 August 1966, having barnacles scraped off her hull on what was one of her last refits before being sold to Long Beach the following year.

Opposite below: Thorneycroft could undertake most ship repair work. Here, the Clan Line's *Clan Ross* is rather dwarfed by the King George V dry dock in January 1976. *Clan Ross* was built in 1966 and is shown here while undertaking conversion to the Union Castle Line's *Kinpurnie Castle*. She was renamed *Kinpurnie Universal* in 1979 and sold to Greece in 1982 as *Syros Reefer*.

The Exormis Shipping Co. MS *Aristides Xilas* in No.7 dry dock on 24 September 1973.

The Normandy ferry *Leopard* during her annual refit in April 1978. Built at Nantes in 1968, she served the Southampton-Le Havre route until 1984. In 1976, the year of this photograph, ownership became P&O Normandy Ferries.

Opposite above: MV *Edinburgh Clipper* entering the King George V dry dock on 2 August 1976.

Opposite below: The motor ships *Discovery* and *John Biscoe* entering dry dock on 28 April 1978. Behind *John Biscoe* is one of the huge Stothert & Pitt-built cranes.

Sealink's *Cuthred* was built in Lowestoft in 1969 at a cost of £275,000. She could carry forty-eight cars and 400 passengers. At 750 tons she was the Isle of Wight's largest car ferry at the time. During her 1977/78 refit she had a hoistable mezzanine car deck installed, bringing the car-carrying capacity up to seventy-two.

Opposite page: QE2 having anti-fouling paint applied during a major refit, *c.*1978. The hi-ab crane being used was lifted down using one of the dockside 50-ton cranes and then removed the same way when the job was done. The size of the six-blade propellers can be clearly seen.

Overleaf, above: This view, from January 1979, perhaps shows best the sheer scale of dry dock facility that Southampton has. The two vessels and the two portakabins inside the dry dock, and the spare set of two propellers for the QE2 at the side of the pumping house can clearly give an indication of the immenseness of the dry dock.

Overleaf, below: Taken three years earlier in 1976, the Trafalgar dry dock and the old Harland & Wolff ship repair facility are shown to their best advantage. The piers in the foreground were once used in conjunction with the BOAC seaplane terminal, with a walkway to the shore. The Itchen bridge nears completion and, under the ferry terminal, was located the Empress dock and its dry dock facilities.

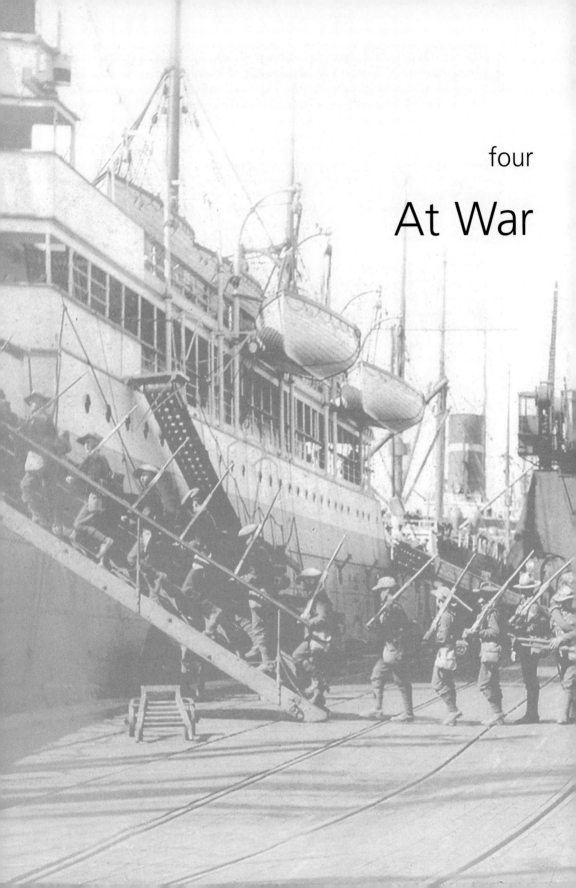

four

At War

From the Crimean War onwards, Southampton has played a major part in wartime. Most importantly, in the Boer War and the First World War, many thousands of troops went off to war from the port. During the trooping season, ships of the P&O and British India fleets took many thousands to and from Egypt, India, Singapore and Hong Kong. During the First World War Southampton was also home to many cross-channel hospital ships as well as to armed merchant cruisers. There was little threat of air attack then and the port was one of the most important to the Allies.

At the start of the Second World War, Southampton was attacked many times by air and the sounds of air-raid sirens could be heard over the city almost daily. The liners all but disappeared for the duration. Their new base was Gourock on the Clyde, with many cargo ships going to Liverpool. Despite the constant threat of air attack, Southampton continued to be used as a major base for ship repair and for the build up to D-Day. From late 1943 onwards the docks were filled with landing craft for the invasion, and seeing tanks and jeeps in the main streets of Southampton was an everyday occurrence. In August 1945, the *Queen Mary* returned to Southampton but still as a troopship. She spent many months transporting war brides to the USA and Canada and, by 1946, although the bomb damage had not been repaired, Southampton was beginning to return to normal.

In the late 1950s, the Government changed from using troopships to transporting soldiers by air instead, and Southampton lost its troopship visits. But, in 1982, the Argentinians invaded the Falklands and ships like the QE2 and *Canberra* were called up as troopships. Much refit work was done in Southampton and on the way to the South Atlantic. Both ships returned safely to a rapturous welcome.

Opposite above: The White Star Dominion Line RMS *Canada* was used as a troopship in both the Boer and First World Wars. She is shown here at Southampton as a Boer War transport. She lasted until 1926 and was scrapped in Italy.

Opposite below: Troops embarking for South Africa on a Union Castle line ship *c.*1905. During the Boer War many ships were commandeered by the Army and the need for troops in South Africa did not subside until the start of the First World War.

MILITARY EMBARKATION SOUTHAMPTON DOCKS   MAX-MILLS

Many German liners were captured in British or Allied ports and were commandeered for troopship service. Here, HMT *Zeppelin* leaves Southampton with allied troops on board.

The Allan liner RMS *Scandinavian* was taken over by the Canadian Pacific Line and was used as a troopship. She is shown here leaving for Canada with dulled down paintwork.

Many hospital ships used Southampton, with the one shown here, HMHS *Youla*, being the smallest. She transported wounded soldiers from the docks to Netley Hospital.

In contrast, this was the largest hospital ship to use Southampton, the almost-50,000grt HMHS *Britannic*. This ship, once the pride of the White Star line fleet, never carried a fare-paying passenger. She was sunk on 21 November 1916 in the Aegean and is the largest ship ever to be sunk in either world war. Here, she is in the Ocean dock being coaled before yet another voyage to Mudros (for Gallipoli) in early 1916.

Above and below: King George V visited the docks on 29 May 1916. He visited No.34 Shed which was being used for transiting wounded soldiers.

Troops embarking onto HMT *Aquitania* in 1916. As a troopship, she could carry over 5,000 soldiers and she was also used as a hospital ship.

As seen from Netley, HMS *Aquitania* enters Southampton Water in 1917 and passes many of the Q-ships (decoy Navy vessels) berthed there.

There was a huge RAMC presence at the docks to serve the many hospital ships and a tented camp was set up in the docks for the medical orderlies.

A fire in one of the sheds behind the International Cold Store in 1916. With many flammable goods in the docks, fire was a great danger.

The Union Castle liner RMS *Carisbrook Castle* was used as a hospital ship from 1914 until the war ended. She had been built in Govan, Glasgow, in 1898 and made the last ever Cape mail steaming from London in 1900. The publisher of this postcard has made the mistake of naming the ship 'Carisbrooke Castle'.

The Royal Mail Steam Packet Co. RMS *Asturias* at Southampton in late 1914.

The city's namesake cruiser HMS *Southampton* on the Clyde in her dazzle-paint camouflage scheme in February 1918.

The Hamburg Amerika steam yacht *Meteor* was a beautiful ship, painted all-over in white. She was ceded to Britain in 1919, painted black and had her bowsprit cut off. She had the indignity of being used as a troopship until 1926, when she was sold to the Norwegian Bergen Steam Ship Co.

The Peninsular & Oriental Steam Navigation Co.'s troopship Assaye leaving the port for India via the Suez Canal in 1923. *Assaye* was built in Greenock as a troopship for £160,860, and was scrapped in 1928 in Stavanger, Norway.

HMT *Somali* outside the International Cold Store. She carries her troopship number on her side. She was used as both a troopship and as a hospital ship. She was laid up in Cornwall in 1923.

Left: HMT *Ettrick* was built in 1938 and was P&O's only permanent troopship. She made her maiden voyage in January 1939 and was sunk on 15 November 1942 after taking part in the North African landings.

Below: The British India Line SS *Nevasa* on troopship duties in the mid–1920s.

Opposite page: Shown here on her lifeboat trials on 2 September 1937, a seaman was injured when he fell onto a boat. The troopship left on her maiden voyage to China on 7 September 1937.

Landing craft in the Test Bay in preparation for the D-Day assault on Normandy. Behind LST 726 is an Irish Sea ferry, converted for carrying landing craft.

The quarterdeck of LST 896.

LST 727 picking up a buoy on Southampton Water in May 1944.

Queen Mary returns from her war service in September 1946, with her sister ship RMS *Queen Elizabeth* in the background.

The paddle steamer *Balmoral* laid up at Northam after her Second World War service.

The rare site of a navy warship in Southampton at Berth No.101 in the mid-1950s.

The Ministry of Transport SS *Empire Windrush* at Southampton in 1948. The *Empire Windrush* was built as the German *Monte Rosa* in 1931 and served as a troopship for Germany during the war. The ship was made famous for bringing the first Caribbean emigrants to Britain after the Second World War.

HMS *Abdiel* was an Exercise Minelayer, built by Thornycroft and launched on 22 January 1967. She was designed to lay exercise minefields, and was commissioned on 17 October 1967. She left the fleet in 1988.

QE2 on her successful return from the Falklands War. Many hundreds of small boats and helicopters came out to welcome the ship from her most arduous journey to date.

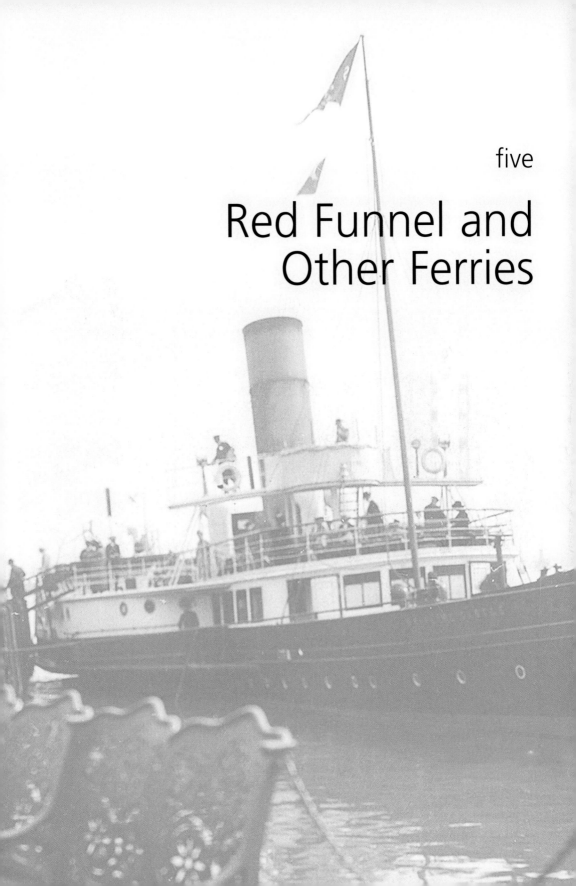

five

Red Funnel and
Other Ferries

It was in 1861 that the Southampton, Isle of Wight & South of England Royal Mail Steam Packet Co. was formed from the Isle of Wight Steam Packet Co. and the Isle of Wight Royal Mail Steam Packet Co. The company, whose name was rapidly shortened to Red Funnel, initially operated seven very small steamers, all named after precious stones. In 1865 it acquired the Isle of Wight & Portsmouth Improved Steamboat Co. and its two paddle steamers. As well as services to the Isle of Wight, the company offered excursion trips along the Hampshire, Dorset and East Sussex coasts.

In 1898, competition, in the form of the Bristol Channel company P&A Campbell, arrived on the Solent and their ship *Cambria*, with its 20kt top speed, caused a stir in the vicinity. Red Funnel was soon to build the *Balmoral* to compete with the new competitor.

During both world wars, Red Funnel was to lose ships to enemy action, most notably *Stirling Castle* off Malta in 1915 and *Gracie Fields* during the Dunkirk evacuation of May 1940.

By the 1960s the paddlers had gone and Red Funnel had returned to its roots as a ferry company between Southampton and Cowes. The company also owned, and still does, a fleet of tugs in and around Southampton.

Opposite above: PS *Stirling Castle* at the Town Quay, *c.*1910. At this time, Red Funnel operated the following fleet: *Solent Queen, Prince of Wales, Duchess of York, Lorna Doone, Balmoral, Queen* (II), *Stirling Castle, Bournemouth Queen* and *Lord Elgin.*

Opposite below: The excursion steamer *Princess Mary* off Cowes, Isle of Wight, *c.*1920.

PRINCESS MARY

Red Funnel's *Lord Elgin* leaves Ryde in May 1938.

An unknown Red Funnel steamer, photographed in the late 1930s at Southampton, with the dock offices visible above her lifeboat.

Passing the Union Castle motor ship, RMS *Dunottar Castle*. A Thames sailing barge is about to be passed too in this late 1930s view of Southampton.

Bournemouth Queen and *Mauretania* (the ex-*Queen*) before the start of the excursion season, most probably at Northam, on 27 March 1936. *Mauretania* was renamed in 1934 when the famous Cunard liner *Mauretania* was sent to the breaker's yard. This was done so that Cunard could retain the name for its new *Mauretania* (II), which was built at Cammell Laird's on the Mersey.

Duchess of Cornwall and *Princess Elizabeth* on 8 August 1938. *Princess Elizabeth* was built at Southampton in 1927 at the yard of Day, Summers & Co.

Bournemouth Queen takes her last sailing into Southampton on 29 August 1957.

Opposite above: The steamer *Medina* on 25 June 1961.

Opposite below: The *Cowes Castle* on her first day of sailing on 21 December 1965.

Norris Castle was an ex-landing craft used as a goods and freight ferry to the Isle of Wight.

The Hythe ferry, PS *Hampton*, at the Town Quay in the 1920s or 1930s.

Hampton passing the empty floating dry dock on its way to the Town Quay from Hythe pier in the mid-1930s.

The Southern Railway ferry, *Hantonia*, in the docks in 1936. As well as the local ferries to the Isle of Wight and Hythe, Southampton was also a major port for ferry services to France and the Channel Islands.

By the late 1960s, Southampton was the major ferry port to Le Havre, Cherbourg, Spain and Gibraltar, with numerous ferry companies sailing on the longer routes. Here, MV *Dragon* leaves the port on 12 July 1967.

The Swedish Lloyd ferry, MV *Patricia*, leaves the port on 28 June 1967.

Opposite above: Saga is shown here on 28 September 1966.

Opposite below: The high-speed *Shearwater 4* hydrofoil passing Fawley on the way to the Isle of Wight on 9 June 1975.

The Isle of Wight Sealink ferry *Freshwater* under repair and overhaul at the Thorneycroft yard in the mid–1970s.

Hovercraft have been a relatively common sight in the port over the years, from the Cunard SRN6 hovercraft (which was loaded onto *Sylvania* at Southampton in 1967) to the numerous fast ferries to the Isle of Wight. This SRN6 No.24 was used as a tender by Cunard from February-April 1967 on fly-sail cruises from Gibraltar.

HOVERSERVICE

DAILY FLIGHTS (except Saturday) TO

BOURNEMOUTH

At 8.50 (not Sunday) and 10.10

Single Fare £1.20 adults   80p children under 14 yrs.
Day Return £1.80   £1.20   „   „

FLIGHT TIME 35 MINUTES

DAILY FLIGHTS (except Saturday) TO

SOUTHAMPTON ROYAL PIER

At 3.05 (not Sunday) and 7.35

Single Fare £1.20 adults   80p children under 14 yrs.
Day Return £1.80   £1.20   „   „

FLIGHT TIME 40 MINUTES

All Flights subject to weather conditions and other circumstances

For further information contact:

West Wight Travel Centre, Freshwater 2559; or Fountain Coaches, Yarmouth 389

TICKETS OBTAINABLE ON BOARD CRAFT

This poster from the late 1970s is for the Hoverservice from the Isle of Wight to Southampton and Bournemouth.

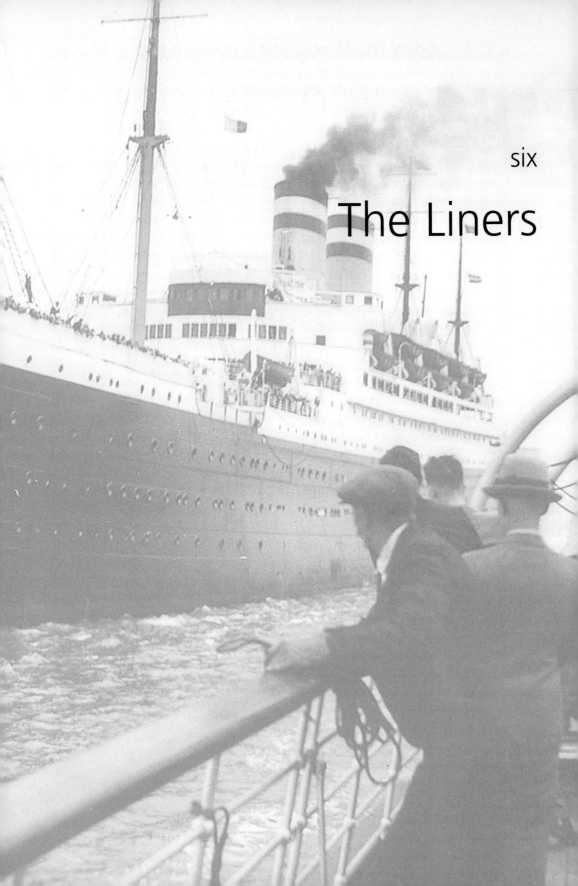

six

The Liners

From the first days of the docks to the present, passenger ships have been an important factor in the port's expansion and development. Many of the dock extensions have been to facilitate the growth in size and number of ocean liners calling at the port. Most of the famous names in British shipping have used Southampton as a base while many foreign lines, realising Southampton's importance, have used it as their British port of call.

Many local men and women worked aboard these liners as stokers, trimmers, greasers, deckhands, stewards, and so on but the port has also seen its share of tragedy, with over half of the crew of the *Titanic*, for example, being residents of the town. Many local people have been employed to service the liners too, from stevedores and porters to workers in the liner laundries and market gardens in and around the city that have supplied clean linen and fresh fruits and vegetables for the multitude of ships of the many lines that used the port.

Southampton saw a huge decline in passenger services in the 1960s and 1970s but from the mid-1980s onwards, growth of passenger traffic through the port has been little short of miraculous. The huge expansion of the cruise ship market, led in Britain by the oldest passenger line still in existence (P&O), has seen the number of ships using the port go up almost five times from 1981 to the present day. Nowadays, only Cunard still operates a traditional transatlantic passenger service, albeit for only a few months per year in the summer, but, as the pictures that follow will testify, Southampton was at one time the premier port in the world, with more calls to more locations than almost any other port. The 'golden age' of liner travel was in the 1930s, with the advent of large, luxurious floating palaces.

Opposite above: The Town Quay in the mid-1920s, with three of the world's largest passenger ships in dock. White Star's *Majestic* and *Homeric* are in the Ocean dock while Cunard's *Berengaria* is in the floating dry dock for overhaul. An unidentified Union Castle ship (perhaps *Balmoral Castle*) is visible too.

Opposite below: From 1924 until the 1930s, one of the truly outstanding sights in the port was the scene shown here – a huge liner in the floating dry dock. Here, the floating dock (the world's largest) is shown lifting the world's largest ship at the time. White Star's *Majestic* weighed in at 56,651 tons an the floating dock could lift her high and dry in less than ten hours.

2K. Town Quay and Docks, Southampton

163. F. G. O. Stuart. R. M. S. "MAJESTIC" (56,551 TONS) THE WORLDS LARGEST LINER,
IN THE WORLDS LARGEST FLOATING DRY-DOCK, SOUTHAMPTON.

Majestic was originally the Hamburg Amerika liner *Bismarck*. Ceded to Britain as war reparation, *Majestic* was an uncompleted hull at the end of the First World War. Finished by her builders, Blohm und Voss, she sailed for Southampton as *Bismarck* in 1921 and was renamed *Majestic* when she arrived at the port. Here, she was readied for transatlantic service as a British ship, the largest vessel in the world at the time. In 1936, she was sold to the Admiralty and went to Rosyth as the cadet ship HMS *Caledonia*.

Opposite above: Perhaps the most famous vessel ever to sail from Southampton was the *Titanic*. In this rare view, she is seen warping out from berth No.43 in the White Star dock. On her aft docking bridge is William McMaster Murdoch, who was to die when she foundered only five days after this view was taken on 10 April 1912.

Opposite below: One of White Star Line's big four, RMS *Cedric* is shown here in the late 1920s. This photograph was taken by one of the engineers on board RMS *Mauretania*. *Cedric* was launched in 1902 and her final voyage was on 5 September 1931 from Liverpool to New York. She was replaced by the motor ship *Britannic* and was sold for scrap in 1932.

Opposite above: The two last White Star Line ships built were the motor ships *Britannic* and *Georgic*. Both were of about 32,000 tons and were built at Harland & Wolff in Belfast. *Britannic* was to be the last White Star ocean liner and was sold for scrap in 1960, after her engines caused major problems in her last few voyages.

Opposite below: Georgic was all but destroyed at Port Tewfik, Egypt, after being attacked by a German bomber during the Second World War. She was rebuilt with one funnel and served until 1956 when she, too, was scrapped. She is shown here in late May 1936.

Photographed from the deck of the *Berengaria* in June 1933, *Mauretania* looks resplendent in her all-over white livery. She was painted in this fetching livery when used for cruising from both Southampton and New York. In 1934, she was laid up in the Western docks after her withdrawal from service. Her white hull soon showed the ravages of years of service and became rust-streaked and grubby. She left Southampton under her own power to be scrapped at Rosyth, stopping at the entrance to the Tyne where she saluted her builders for the last time.

In March 1936, Cunard White Star's new flagship, RMS *Queen Mary*, entered Southampton for the very first time to enter dry dock to have her hull checked, cleaned and painted. She passed, in the Western docks, Union Castle's *Windsor Castle*, Cunard White Star's *Majestic* and the Southern Railway ferry *Hampton Ferry* (which had been chartered for the event. The scaffolding at the right of *Queen Mary* was for the many press photographers who wanted to capture the momentous event of the world's largest liner in the world's largest graving dock.

In August 1939 a new *Mauretania* entered service. Destined to make only one voyage before war started, she was a frequent sight in Southampton from the post-war period onwards. Here, she visits the port in May 1955.

Cunard's 'Green Goddess', RMS *Caronia*, sets sail for America in the late 1940s with the tug *Gladstone* in attendance. *Caronia* was built especially for cruising although she undertook transatlantic sailings from Southampton to New York too. For most of her life she was painted in four shades of green. When built, she also had the distinction of the world's largest-ever funnel. She foundered off Guam and was a total loss.

RMS *Ivernia*, one of the mid-1950s quartet of liners built by John Brown's at Clydebank for the Canadian service, is shown leaving the port in *c.*1960.

Cunard shore staff watch as *Caronia* sails on 2 July 1966 for New York where she embarked North Cape cruise passengers. She was the first ship to sail after the end of the Seamen's Strike of that year. In the distance is the *Queen Elizabeth*, which sailed later the same day.

Opposite above: Strikes were a major problem in the 1960s and were responsible for the rapid decline of the British merchant fleet, and certainly killed any chance that the transatlantic liners may have had of competing with the airlines. Passengers deserted the shipping lines in droves and never returned. In little more than a year Cunard's *Queen Mary* had been sold.

This view shows Cunard office staff standing in for striking stevedores on 9 May 1967 as they unload the *Queen Mary* during a wildcat strike. In the background is a truck of Liners Laundry Ltd.

Opposite below: One of the very few recent views in this book is this one of my two favourite modern liners at the port for the last time in 2002. The two ships, Cunard's QE2 and P&O's *Victoria*, were the last two ocean liners to be built in Scotland. *Victoria* (the ex-*Kungsholm* of Swedish America Line) was about to be sold to become Holiday Kreuzfarten's *Mona Lisa*.

R.M.S. "BALMORAL CASTLE."

Opposite above: Union Castle Line's RMS *Kenilworth Castle* at the new extension to the Itchen Quays in *c.*1908. She was built in 1904 at Belfast and was broken up in 1936. *Kenilworth Castle* was 570ft 6in long and was capable of 14kt. In 1918, while proceeding up the English Channel, the ship collided with HMS *Rival.* Several depth charges were dropped and exploded under the hull and fifteen people were killed.

Opposite below: Balmoral Castle, photographed in 1936, was constructed by the Fairfield Ship Building & Engineering Co. at Govan in 1910. In October of that year she carried the Duke of Connaught to South Africa for the opening of Parliament and was given yellow funnels and masts for this voyage. In 1939, she was scrapped.

Windsor Castle was launched on 9 March 1922 at Clydebank by the Prince of Wales. Interestingly, a small river Severn steamer of the same name had to be purchased and renamed by Union Castle to free the name for the liner. Rebuilt with extended bow and two funnels in 1937, she was sunk by a torpedo bomber on 23 March 1943 in the Mediterranean. Here, she is seen on her normal Test Quay berth, next to the International Cold Storage warehouse in the late 1920s.

Windsor Castle (II) in January 1938 after her return to service after her major re-building. After rebuilding her passenger complement was 219 First Class, 191 Second Class and 194 Third Class.

Opposite above: Dunottar or *Dunvegan Castle* being fuelled at the Union Castle Line's berths in 1937. The two ships both entered service as intermediate steamers in 1936 but could, if required, reach Cape Town in mail steamer passage time. *Dunottar* was sold to Incres Line in 1958, becoming their *Victoria* and made her initial cruise to the Mediterranean on 14 December 1959, while *Dunvegan* was torpedoed off Ireland on 27 August 1940.

Opposite below: Carnarvon Castle (II) was launched in Belfast on 14 January 1926 and made her maiden voyage from Southampton on 16 July that year. In 1938 she was modernised with a single funnel. In 1947, she inaugurated the post-war emigrant service to South Africa and was broken up in Japan in 1962. This view dates from *c.*1930.

Above: A post-war shot taken from the end of Mayflower Park of a Union Castle liner leaving for the Cape.

Opposite above: A trio of Union Castle Line ships in the Western docks, c.1950. *Arundel Castle* is the bottom ship, while at the top of the picture are Cunard's *Queen Elizabeth* (in the King George V graving dock), *Queen Mary*, being fuelled, and either a Bergen Line ship or an NYK one behind her. It was a very rare occurrence for the two Cunard superliners to be in dock together.

Opposite below: Launched in October 1947, RMS *Edinburgh Castle* (the third ship to carry the name) entered service in December 1948 with a maiden voyage from Southampton to Cape Town and Durban. In 1962, about two years after this view was taken, she was rebuilt with a single mast. She made her last passenger sailing on 5 March 1976, with one cargo voyage to the Cape after this. On 3 June 1976, she arrived at Kaohsiung, Taiwan, for breaking by Chin Tai Steel Enterprises.

Opposite above: During the 1966 Seamen's Strike, many ships were laid up at Southampton, including this Union Castle trio at Berth 101. *Good Hope Castle*, almost brand new at the time, is on the left. Designed as a fast cargo vessel, she was the second but last ship built for Union Castle, and had twelve passenger berths added in 1967 so she could serve the remote Atlantic outpost of St Helena. In 1978 she was sold to Costa Armatori SpA of Genoa and renamed *Paola C.*

Opposite below: The SS *Reina del Mar* was built for the Pacific Steam Navigation Co. and launched in 1955. In 1963, she was chartered as a cruise ship to the Travel Savings Association and managed by Union Castle. With accommodation for 1,047 she proved very popular and Union Castle purchased her in 1973. In 1975, she was sold prematurely to Tung Cheng Steel, Kaohsiung, Taiwan, for breaking – a casualty of the 1974 oil crisis that saw the loss of many older liners. This view was taken in November 1966.

Below: One of the first passenger lines to use the port of Southampton was the Peninsular & Oriental Steam Navigation Co. The line moved its main services to London in the nineteenth century and it was not until the late 1920s that regular services were undertaken from Southampton again. The company's main base in the UK is now Southampton and its cruise ships regularly leave the port for warmer and sunnier climes. Here, RMS *Strathnaver*, one of the original 'White Sisters', is shown in the port in 1935, most likely leaving on a Mediterranean on Norwegian Fjords cruise.

Above: A trio of P&O ships are shown in this aerial view of the docks in the early 1960s. RMS *Iberia* is in the dry dock, with one of the two Elders & Fyffes cruise ships (*Camito* or *Golfito*) berthed next to the entrance, while two other P&O liners and one of the British India vessels (*Uganda* or *Kenya*) is berthed on the extreme right.

Opposite below: The last passenger liner built at Harland & Wolff in Belfast was *Canberra*. Shown here leaving Southampton on her maiden voyage to Australia in 1961, she was a perennial favourite of passengers and crew alike. Converted for cruising, she was sold to Indian breakers in 1997 after a career of thirty-six years, during which she served as a hospital and troopship in the Falklands War, entering the war zone and being caught in the thick of the fighting for Port Stanley. It was here that she earned her nick-name of 'the Great White Whale'. She returned from the war, rust-streaked and battle weary, to a hero's welcome at Southampton.

Oriana leaves the docks soon after her entry to service. She led a chequered life, seving for P&O and being sold into preservation in China. She spent many years in Shanghai before being moved to Dalien. In 2005, after she was capsized at her berth during a storm, she made her last ever voyage to an Indian beach, where she was cut up.

Iberia was 719ft 9in long and was of 29,779grt. Built in 1954, she is shown here at Southampton on 8 June 1972. She was sold to Taiwan breakers and dismantled at Kaohsiung.

Above: British India's SS *Nevasa* at Berth 101 in the mid-1950s.

Above: Canadian Pacific's RMS *Empress of Australia* leaving Southampton in 1931 or 1932 on a Norwegian Fjord cruise. Dressed overall in flags she makes an impressive sight. Launched in 1913 for the Hamburg Amerika Line, she was originally named *Admiral von Tirpitz*. In February 1914, her name was changed to just plain *Tirpitz*. Uncompleted before the start of the war, she was laid up and finished in 1919. Handed over to the British as war reparation, she arrived in Hull with *Kaiserine Auguste Victoria* and was used for trooping by P&O. On 25 July 1921 she was purchased by Canadian Pacific and named *Empress of China*. She was renamed *Empress of Australia* by CPR in June 1922. After a long career (including use as a royal yacht twice), she was broken up at Inverkeithing in 1952.

Right: Painting the stern of Canadian Pacific's largest ever passenger ship, the Clydebuilt RMS *Empress of Britain*, at Southampton in 1936.

Opposite below: The Orient Line's RMS *Orford* in Southampton Water in the early 1930s. As well as running to Australia, she also performed many cruises from the UK, most notably from Southampton and Immingham during the Depression years of the early 1930s.

RMS *Parana* in the Empress docks, *c.*1906. She was constructed in 1904 by Workman Clark in Belfast. On 10 September 1917, she was attacked by a German submarine and fought for over ninety minutes, firing seventy shells in reply to over 100 from the U-boat. She survived the engagement and was broken up in 1933.

Opposite above: An evening snapshot of Southampton in the mid-1930s, with *Empress of Britain* on the left. *Empress of Britain* was sunk by U-32 on 28 October 1940 and was the single largest shipping loss of the Second World War.

Opposite below: One of the first shipping lines to make Southampton its home was the Royal Mail Steam Packet Co. in 1840. This was a tradition that was to last until 1980, although the Royal Mail name had all but disappeared in 1972 with a reorganisation of its owners, Furness Withy. *Arlanza*, shown here, was built for the Southampton-River Plate service in 1911 and scrapped in 1938 at Blyth, Northumberland. 1,700 guests came to say farewell at Montevideo on her last call to the port in August of that year.

The largest motor ship in the world when built, RMS *Asturias* was launched in 1925 and was also the first cruiser-sterned ship for Royal Mail. Her 1926 maiden voyage was from Southampton-River Plate. Re-engined with oil fueled steam turbines in 1934, she was torpedoed in 1943. Salvaged in 1945, she was taken over by the Government as an emigrant carrier and was involved as a troopship during the Korean War. In 1957, she was broken up at Faslane, but not before being used as a set in the film *A Night to Remember*, perhaps the best film ever made about the tragedy of the *Titanic*.

In the late 1950s, Shaw Savill planned the construction of two new liners for their round-the-world service. They were the revolutionary *Southern Cross* and *Northern Star*, both rear engined to ensure plenty of cargo and passenger space amidships. Above is *Southern Cross*, while right is a ticket to view the maiden voyage of *Northern Star* on 10 July 1962.

N⁰ 822

BRITISH TRANSPORT COMMISSION
SOUTHAMPTON DOCKS

MAIDEN VOYAGE
S.S. "NORTHERN STAR"
10th JULY 1962.
SAILING 30/31 BERTH — 3 p.m.

The "Holder" is permitted, subject to the conditions stated on the back hereof, to enter Southampton Docks as from 1.0 p.m. and proceed to the SPECTATORS ENCLOSURE at BERTHS 30/31 to witness the sailing of the s.s. "Northern Star".

S. A. FINNIS,
Chief Docks Manager

ADMIT ONE ONLY
Cars Not Admitted

Opposite below: Launched at Belfast on 8 May 1913 as RMS *Andes*, this ship made her maiden voyage from Liverpool-Valparaiso for Pacific Steam Navigation Co., a sister line to Royal Mail. In 1929, she was painted all-over white and converted to the cruising steamer *Atlantis*. She served successfully through two world wars, being used in the first as an armed merchant cruiser, helping sink the German commerce raider *Greif*, and in the second as a hospital ship and troopship. Between 1939–46, she sailed 280,000 miles and carried 35,000 wounded. She is shown here leaving Southampton on her penultimate voyage on 26 September 1951. She was laid up on the Clyde and broken at Faslane in 1952.

S.S. JAN PIETERSZOON COEN. SOUTHAMPTON 1924

MARNIX V.S. ALDEGONDE

Holland America's SS *Nieuw Amsterdam* enters Southampton on 12 August 1964, en route from Rotterdam to New York.

Opposite above: For many Dutch lines, their main port of call in the UK was Southampton. Rotterdam Lloyd, Nederland Royal Mail Lines and Holland America used the port. Here, the SS *Jan Pietbrszoon Coen* is shown leaving the port in 1924.

Opposite below: The Rotterdam Lloyd liner SS *Marnix V.S. Aldegonde* leaves Southampton in the mid-1930s for the Netherlands East Indies.

THE IMPERATOR. THE NEW HAMBURG AMERICAN LINER.

ALBERT BALLIN

North German Lloyd's *Columbus*, a sister ship to White Star's RMS *Homeric* (herself, war reparation) is tendered off Ryde on 11 August 1933.

Opposite above: In April 1913, barely a year after the loss of the world's largest ship, the new contender for the crown entered Southampton on her maiden voyage to New York from Hamburg. The new ship, the SS *Imperator*, is shown here passing Ryde on a photograph by W.R. Hogg. While she was the largest ship in the world, *Imperator* was not the longest and she had a giant eagle figurehead constructed on her bow to reclaim that record. Sadly, a storm in the Atlantic put paid to her claims when the figurehead was destroyed by the power of wind and wave.

Opposite below: Many foreign liners did not sail all of the way into the dock system, preferring to be tendered off Ryde or Cowes by the port's passenger and cargo tenders. Hamburg Amerika's SS *Albert Ballin* (named after the designer of the trio of *Imperator*, *Vaterland* and *Bismarck*) is being tendered off Cowes in the late 1920s by a Red Funnel paddle steamer.

Here, the Hamburg Amerika *Frankfurt* (built in 1954 and of 8,959grt) is shown here being tendered on 15 June 1960 by *Calshot*, and an unknown tug, which is filled with mail sacks.

Opposite above: Perhaps the most glamorous of all ocean liners was the French Line SS *Normandie*. The only serious competitor to the *Queen Mary* on the North Atlantic, both ships fought valiantly to win the Blue Riband. This view of *Normandie*, off Ryde, shows her flying the pennant for winning the Blue Riband on her aft mast. The ship never came into the port itself, ordinarily being tendered by Red Funnel paddle steamers while anchored off Ryde.

Opposite below: Spiritual successor to *Normandie* was the French Line's SS *France*. Making her maiden voyage in 1961, *France* was a common sight into Southampton in the 1960s. She was sold to become the world's largest cruise ship, the SS *Norway*, and spent many years on Caribbean cruises. She made her last call to Southampton in late 2001. She has recently been towed to an unknown future in Malaysia after being laid up at Bremerhaven for over a year after a fatal boiler explosion. She is shown here off Hamble in 1968.

Opposite above: The *Regina Magna* of International Cruises SA, Panama, on 8 June 1972, berthed at the Western docks.

Opposite below: Blacklegs coaling the American Line's USMS (United States Mail Ship) *St Paul* in 1911. The coal strike of that year caused many problems with the shipping lines and many transatlantic liners carried coal in their passenger accommodation while travelling from the USA to the UK, to ensure they had enough coal to return westwards again. *St Paul* rammed HMS *Gladiator* in 1904, sinking the navy ship with the loss of almost all on board.

Above: Dressed overall in flags, the United States Line's SS *George Washington* passes Cowes in the mid-1920s.

Right and overleaf: When built as *Vaterland* for Hamburg Amerika, she was the largest ship in the world and was only surpassed by her sister ship, *Bismarck*. Laid up in New York at the start of the First World War, *Vaterland* was commandeered by the Americans and converted to the troopship USS *Leviathan*. After numerous trips bringing troops to and from France, Leviathan was handed over to the United States Line and was a regular caller at the port until the mid-1930s. Laid up in New York after various fires on board, she was sent to Rosyth to be broken next to her two sisters, *Imperator* (*Berengaria*) and *Bismarck* (*Majestic*).

Above: The last great United States liner was the mighty Big 'U', the SS *United States*. Built at Newport News in Virginia as a superliner/hospital ship/troopship, she was designed to be converted within forty-eight hours from one to another. Her top speed was in excess of 35kt and she exceeded this speed on her maiden voyage to take the Blue Riband. She is shown here entering Southampton Water after that record-breaking first trip. She left service in 1969, but has been laid up ever since. She survives today, owned by Norwegian Cruise Line, but is an empty hulk located in Philadelphia, in the USA. It is said that the only wood on board ship was the Steinway piano and the butcher's block.

The flying boat G-AGEU *Hampshire* at the BOAC terminal at Southampton docks in 1950. In the pre-war period, flying boats were a common sight at the port. The Imperial Airways Empire flying boats used the area off Hythe pier. Post-war, a new terminal was built for the flying boats. In the background is the *Queen Elizabeth*. As well as the BOAC flying boats, flights were made by Aquila Airways in the early 1950s.

The BOAC terminal and the Hythe ferry, *c.*1949. At the ocean dock are, from left to right: Cunard's *Caronia* and *Queen Elizabeth*. By the mid-1950s, the flying boats had gone, but the remains of their piers were still in place until the 1980s.

142

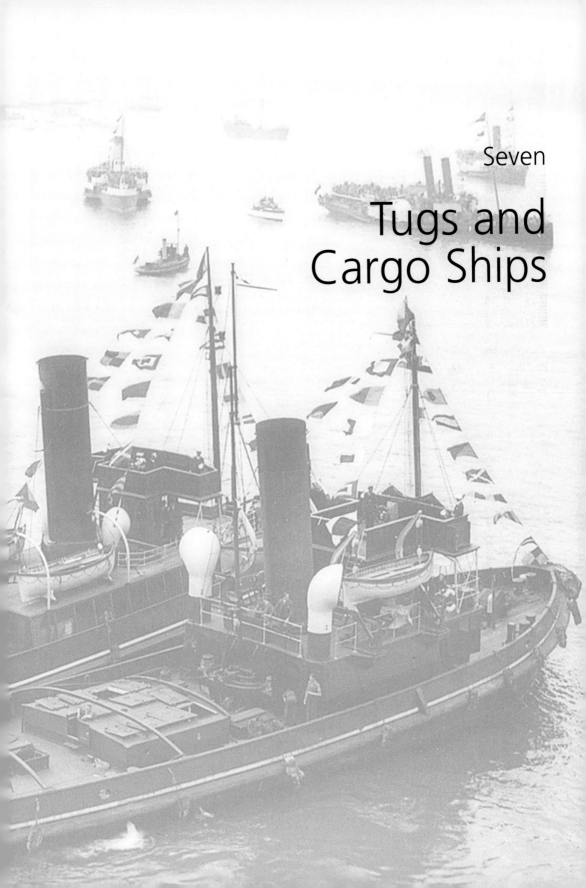

Seven

Tugs and Cargo Ships

Although Southampton has been the country's premier passenger port since the 1840s, it has also been an important cargo port. Many of the old liners carried up to 10,000 tons of cargo, from refrigerated cargo/passenger liners carrying frozen meat from Australia, New Zealand and South America to specie (gold and silver bullion) across the Atlantic and even cattle, horses and other animals from around the world. Many of the liner companies, from Union Castle and the Royal Mail Steam Packet Co. to Cunard and White Star, carried a huge quantity of goods to and from Britain. In fact, many carried much more than is realised today and some liners (*Titanic* included – which carried a new Renault car to the USA) carried cars and small aircraft and other high-value items. Many cargo ships used the port too. From new potatoes and tomatoes from the Channel Islands to wool from Australia and cotton from Egypt, bananas from the Canary Islands and the Caribbean to oil and other fuels to Fawley refinery, the port has seen many different types of goods. The docks were well provided to handle the many different products that came into the port. Today, most cargo is containerised but the port is also one of the major ports for the import and export of motor cars. It is a common sight to see car transporters full of new Land Rovers, Minis and Peugeots being exported while many new (and grey import) Japanese vehicles are imported via Southampton.

Tugs did, and still do, play an important part in the dock system. With the introduction of Azimuth propulsion pods and bow thrusters on many modern ships, they are needed less often than they used to be but Red Funnel still has a fleet of tugs at the port.

Opposite above: Tugs pull White Star's RMS *Olympic* into the docks in September 1911, when she was rammed by the light cruiser HMS *Hawke. Olympic* was badly damaged but was repaired temporarily at Southampton before being sailed to Belfast for permanent repair. It was this repair work that caused her sister *Titanic* to be late and set off for her maiden voyage on 10 April 1912, instead of in March.

Opposite below: The tug/tender *Romsey* was brand new in 1930. Painted in white, a colour she was in only in her maiden year, she escorts RMS *Majestic* on 14 August of that year.

Photographed from the *Queen Mary* are three of the tugs which pulled her out of the ocean dock on 27 May 1936 as she left for New York on her maiden voyage. Dressed overall in flags, they are watched by some of the many pleasure steamers and small boats that flocked to the port on that day to watch Southampton's most famous liner leave on the very first of her 1,001 transatlantic crossings.

Pictured in the Ocean dock in March 1938 is the tug *Greetings*.

Romsey, shown here fully loaded and probably tendering a large liner, was of 509 tons displacement. Her wireless call sign was GSKM.

The tug/tender *Flying Breeze* in 1960.

Gladstone in the Western docks in 1960.

Opposite above: The French Chargeur Reunis SS *Groix* at the Western docks on 10 May 1951. Built in 1922, she was scraped by shipbreakers in Bordeaux.

Opposite below: The SS *Jamaica Merchant* was a banana ship which made her maiden voyage in 1935 from Southampton to Kingston, Montego Bay, Oracassa, Port Morant, Kingston, Rotterdam and back to Southampton. The banana ships of Elders & Fyffes and United Fruit Co. were once a very common sight in the port.

Overleaf: The dredger *Sandswift* and a Red Funnel ferry in the docks in the early 1970s. Behind the ferry is a lightship, probably *Calshot*, which is now land-locked and encased in concrete at Ocean Village.

Opposite above: Photographed in the late 1950s from what is still an excellent ship-spotting vantage point at Mayflower Park is the MV *Philipia*.

Opposite below: Esso Cheyenne at Fawley, 19 July 1948. The oil tanker was built in 1942, was of 9,798 tons and had a top speed of 10½kt.

Esso Dublin in Southampton Water, 3 September 1951.

The tanker *Winchester* at Fawley, 3 September 1951.

Waterman Steamship Corporation's SS *Wacosta* and *Flying Breeze* at berths Nos 32-33 on 12 August 1964.

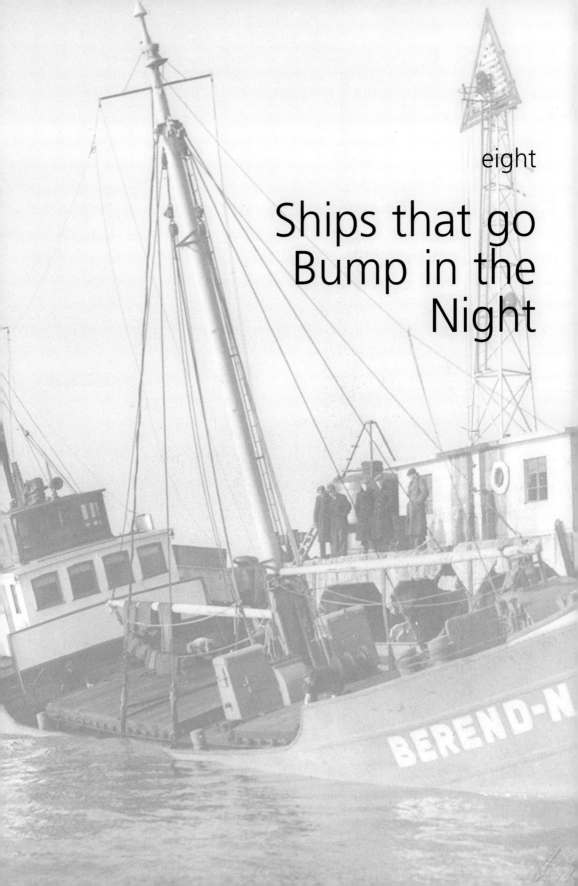

eight

Ships that go Bump in the Night

With its extensive ship-repair yards, Southampton was well-placed to repair many of the ships that were damaged by collision, running aground or fire, and repairs could often be undertaken speedily and cheaply at the port. Even today, despite modern safety technology, advances in radar and safer ships, accidents still occur. Within the following pages are pictures of just some of those accidents that have happened over the years in and around the dock system.

The London & South Western Railway ferry SS *Vera*, being towed back into Southampton on 22 March 1901 after a collision with the SS *Simla*.

Opposite above: HMS P.32 towing the British India Steam Navigation Co.'s SS *Waipara* into the port after she was torpedoed in the English Channel.

Opposite below: The entrance to the docks was heavily mined by the Germans during the Second World War and stray mines were still a danger well into the 1950s. The Dutch vessel SS *Nigerstroom* was a casualty of a mine in 1946. She is shown here listing heavily to port with a gaping hole in her side caused by the mine.

Carrying timber was often a dangerous occupation. The cargo, piled high on the open decks, often shifted and could cause ships to founder. SS *Springdale* has luckily managed to reach port safely in 1947, despite the severe list to port. Unloading the cargo of timber after the ship had listed like this was also a dangerous proposition and it was not unknown for a ship to capsize at the dockside.

The tanker *Petros* at Southampton after collision in the Channel in 1952.

The cargo ship *Reserv* after collision in Southampton Water in 1952.

The shallows and mudflats on the entry to Southampton Water often caused problems for ships entering the port. Even the Cunard RMS *Queen Elizabeth* spent a scary night trapped on a mudbank in the late 1940s. Here, *Berend-N* is shown after grounding at Calshot in 1953.

THE "OLYMPIC" AT S'AMPTON   'X' WHERE SHE WAS RAM'D BY 'HAWKE'

S CRIBB

OLYMPIC COLLISION.

Above: The *Olympic* entering dock after her collision with HMS *Hawke* in September 1911. The damage is marked on this original 1911 postcard just below the poop deck well area.

Left: A clear view of the damage done to *Olympic* after the collision. The damage required a return to Belfast for repairs, the Thompson Dry Dock there being the only one large enough to accomodate the new superliner. A diver is already in the water inspecting the extensive damage below the waterline. *Olympic* is the author's favourite vessel, and the brass from one of the portholes resides at home, made into a scale model of the ship by Thomas Ward, the company that broke her up.